www.providencebooks.net

Publisher Contact

Email:contact@providencebooks.net

Social media: facebook.com/providencebooks

Acknowledgements

The team at Providence Books would like to thank our friends, family, suppliers and customers for making our vision of creating the highest-quality books a reality. Thanks for purchasing and enjoy the quotes!

This page is intentionally left blank

This page is intentionally left blank

A good artist is willing to die many times over. What's funny is, I've died so many times.

Billy Corgan

All I can go on is my own value system.

Billy Corgan

As a citizen of the great city of Chicago, I find it impossible to root against the White Sox. The White Sox organization has been much more consistent, in my lifetime at least, at putting a winning ballclub on the field.

Billy Corgan

Calm, open debate, and logical thought drive strength to its maximum effectiveness.

Billy Corgan

Compliments and criticism are all ultimately based on some form of projection.

Billy Corgan

Do I belong in the conversation about the best artists in the world? My answer is yes, I do.

Billy Corgan

Even if you don't believe in God, exploring fully the idea of a god or gods should pose no threat to you.

Billy Corgan

For someone who's had the level of success I've had, there's been very little critical review of my work, which is pretty fascinating.

Billy Corgan

Hey, Christian rock, if you want to be good, stop copying U2. U2 already did it. You know what I mean? There's a lot of U2-esque Christian rock.

Billy Corgan

I always thought Kurt Cobain was the perfect embodiment of the great alternative guitar player.

Billy Corgan

I believe that if the Tribune company ever tries to close down Wrigley Field that you will have a protest from every corner of the globe.

Billy Corgan

I did 13-something years of talking to wrestlers and promoters about why they did certain things and why they booked matches a certain way and what they were thinking and whether they were satisfied with the draw. And I got a lot of insight in the business.

Billy Corgan

I didn't find Jesus. He's been there the whole time.

Billy Corgan

I didn't grow up with my mother, and so losing her for real was like, some sort of latent childhood, some sort of unresolved issue. When she left for real, it was sort of like, I was done.

Billy Corgan

I do not think wrestling is going to save the world.

Billy Corgan

I do not trust those who make the vaccines, or the apparatus behind it all to push it on us through fear.

Billy Corgan

I don't have a problem with 'Idol' or 'X Factor,' I have a problem with when those things are not given the proper contextual hue.

Billy Corgan

I don't have any sentimental notion about how people are going to remember me.

Billy Corgan

I don't have to play by these rules or do these things... I can actually have my own kind of version.

Billy Corgan

I don't think people are fans of me because I wrote hit songs. I think they're fans because I'm a lunatic or a weirdo. The hit songs came out of my idiosyncratic personality, not the other way around.

Billy Corgan

I don't think people buy records because of anything that happens on Facebook. They buy records cause they're friends say 'I bought this record and I love it.'

Billy Corgan

I don't wanna play this kind of cartoon character anymore.

Billy Corgan

I don't want to be a dead hero.

Billy Corgan

I feel like I'm always fighting not to repeat myself.

Billy Corgan

I grew up in a house of no love or emotion - it kind of sticks with you.

Billy Corgan

I grew up in the suburbs and basically associate the suburbs with cultural death.

Billy Corgan

I had concussions as a kid playing football and basketball, and know what it feels like and to have someone say 'Just rub some dirt on it, and get back in there.'

Billy Corgan

I had such a big mouth for so long that it doesn't faze anybody anymore.

Billy Corgan

I have a saying, which is, 'Crazy is good for business.' I think rock and roll really is about being a bit crazy.

Billy Corgan

I just don't want to live in the past. I'm really disappointed by so many people of my generation who - in order to promote their new work, they have to constantly lean on their past. I don't want to be that type of artist... I see a lot of people out here doing really marginal music.

Billy Corgan

I lay a lot of blame at the feet of Dusty Baker for not being more strict about fundamentals, which I think would give the team a stronger day-to-day identity.

Billy Corgan

I look at other members of my generation who have basically done one thing, and one thing well, and have been handsomely rewarded for it.

Billy Corgan

I mean my point as an artist is I'm on my own little weird journey across the sky here and whether or not anybody's listening, or listening to the degree I would like them to, at the end of the day has to be an inconsequential thing because I can't chase this culture.

Billy Corgan

I mean there's certainly a lot of progressive rock and metal that exists at the underground level, which has its own vitality, as it should. But it seems to have lost its ability to really charge up the hill.

Billy Corgan

I never wanted to leave the Smashing Pumpkins. That was never the plan.

Billy Corgan

I often have deer on my property and there's a fox and owls. You're not going to see that in the city.

Billy Corgan

I realize I'm a mirror.

Billy Corgan

I started thinking that if post modernism is about people opening up all their skeletons, I'm going the other way. I don't want anyone knowing anything about me anymore.

Billy Corgan

I tend to be reactionary.

Billy Corgan

I think God is the most unexplored territory in rock and roll music.

Billy Corgan

I think I'm an artistic radical, and I think I'll be recognized as one. I'm a really good musician and a songwriter, but I think my real legacy will be as a radical.

Billy Corgan

I think a spiritual journey is not so much a journey of discovery. It's a journey of recovery. It's a journey of uncovering your own inner nature. It's already there.

Billy Corgan

I think long and hard about what it is I'm actually trying to do, and then I kind of have to narrow my focus into that. If I don't, I'm too all over the place.

Billy Corgan

I think rock & roll has prepared me for a lot of flexibility.

Billy Corgan

I think the days of working with producers in the conventional sense are over for me.

Billy Corgan

I think when I listen to old records, it puts me back in the atmosphere of what it felt like to make the record and who was there and what the room looked like. It's more a sensory memory.

Billy Corgan

I walked away from going to church when I was 8. I didn't set foot in another church until I was 28.

Billy Corgan

I was brought up Roman Catholic. I'm not even baptized.

Billy Corgan

I was fantasising about my own death, I started thinking what my funeral would be like and what music would be played, I was at that level of insanity.

Billy Corgan

I was part of a generation that changed the world, and it was taken over by posers.

Billy Corgan

I was raised a Christian, but I wouldn't call myself a Christian now. I think when I was younger it was easier to focus on the negative, nihilist vision... this is sort of picking up on the other half of the body, which is God and white light.

Billy Corgan

I was trying to be this person who is cool, eternally rocking.

Billy Corgan

I went to see a shaman. He put his hands on me, and I cried like a baby for an hour.

Billy Corgan

I work differently than most people.

Billy Corgan

I'd reached a point where there was a direct conflict between what I was trying to be and who I really was.

Billy Corgan

I'll come in with a string of riffs and direct the musical ideas. But you still need a band and their input to make the ideas come alive. You can't underestimate band chemistry.

Billy Corgan

I'm a bit weird.

Billy Corgan

I'm a really honest person.

Billy Corgan

I'm attacking the pomposity that says this is more valuable than that. I'm sick of that.

Billy Corgan

I'm definitely responsible for coming in with some basic chord changes, or ideas. Everybody in the band looks to me to come up with the basic seed, so it's not very productive to come in with nothing.

Billy Corgan

I'm from a lower middle class background; all my family were immigrants.

Billy Corgan

I'm not interested in pop art.

Billy Corgan

I'm prepared to spend the rest of my life playing clubs, if that means I'm playing music that I believe in.

Billy Corgan

I'm sort of like a lame, single guy in a red sports car.

Billy Corgan

I'm very disappointed in my country right now, because I think we've kind of lost our moral compass.

Billy Corgan

I'm viewed as this weird, crippled character. But you got to take your lumps.

Billy Corgan

I've always been spiritual but I've never had a proper context, and it took me awhile to find the proper context. It's hard to realize you can have any kind of relationship with God you want... and so I now have a punk rock relationship with God.

Billy Corgan

I've been too productive for too long, and despite what anybody wants to strip away from me, I am influential. I am.

Billy Corgan

I've never had coffee. I've always hated the smell. It was always tea. I was a pretty typical kid, though. I grew up drinking Lipton. I didn't know there was other tea to drink.

Billy Corgan

I've seen foreigners really shift on their view of America, and that's hard for me to take.

Billy Corgan

If I have resistance to something, it means there's something wrong. The resistance to me is a sign of fear.

Billy Corgan

If I worried about appearances, I wouldn't be at Cubs games.

Billy Corgan

If you don't fit into this kind of like gossipy, trendy, Web-hit thingy, you're relegated to sort of second-class celebrity status.

Billy Corgan

In a weird kind of way, music has afforded me an idealism and perfectionism that I could never attain as me.

Billy Corgan

In my case I don't mind playing a character that irritates people or makes people question my sanity.

Billy Corgan

In my particular instance, I came from a family that didn't have anything. Everything I earned in life I made. Myself. With songs that I wrote.

Billy Corgan

In our lives in a lot of ways it's all about fake. You've got people wanting things for fake reasons.

Billy Corgan

In the beginning, though, I have to admit that I did have a chip on my shoulder. I did want to prove everyone wrong. But after I went through the process and came out the other side, it wasn't about anyone else.

Billy Corgan

Indie world won't have me, and mainstream world treats me like an alien, but here I am still floating between these two worlds.

Billy Corgan

Injuries are nothing to be ashamed about.

Billy Corgan

It's a simple formula for me now, I don't play any song I don't want to play.

Billy Corgan

It's important for people to talk and get beyond the wall of Facebook and social media.

Billy Corgan

James, that's a bad situation. I'm not saying it's not repairable, but it's pretty far. When you go from being in one of the best bands in the world to some cover band... as far as I'm concerned, he was playing down at the pub.

Billy Corgan

Jesus teaches us to forgive and I've got to trust him on that one.

Billy Corgan

Like any good tree that one would hope to grow, we must set our roots deep into the ground so that what is real will prosper in the Light of Love.

Billy Corgan

More than any audience in the world, Americans will cross their arms, stare at you and say, 'OK, whaddya got?' - no matter how many times you've proven it to them.

Billy Corgan

Most great records really start with the drums.

Billy Corgan

Most of my arguments with musicians through the years have had more to do with their attitude about music, or their attitude about their own lives, or their personal responsibility. Music has never really been the big centerpiece of the fight.

Billy Corgan

Most people are living lives of sort of survival. And constantly posing an existential crisis, either through fantasy or oblivion, really has been pretty much explored in rock and roll. At least in the western version of rock n' roll.

Billy Corgan

Most people don't know that wrestling came out of the circus.

Billy Corgan

Music is your guide.

Billy Corgan

My father was a guitar player, and I was raised with a super high standard of what good guitar playing was.

Billy Corgan

My mother and I parting company at four years old is a recurring theme; although it's not symbolically necessarily present, it's present in all my relationships.

Billy Corgan

My pat line about the Cubs and payroll is that the amount of merchandise the Cubs would sell off a world series championship would more than cover for a big payroll.

Billy Corgan

My step-mom would tell me that she would get complaints from adults that I stared too much at them.

Billy Corgan

My version, of course, is not this flag-waving, let's all get on the Jesus train and ride out of hell. I'm not that kind of guy. It's an embrace that life is good, worth living and yeah, it's not easy, but there are more pluses than minuses.

Billy Corgan

One thing I've learned to appreciate as I've gotten a little older is direct forms of communication.

Billy Corgan

People think I take some sort of masochistic pleasure out of putting out music that's gonna be unpopular.

Billy Corgan

People try to make a big deal, like I don't want to play my old songs. That's not it. I don't want to play my old songs if that's my only option. That's a different thing.

Billy Corgan

Personally, I think Jesus would like better bands.

Billy Corgan

Radiohead and Our Lady Peace are doing the seven layers of guitar, and I kind of jumped on that before anyone else did.

Billy Corgan

Rock & roll is not about what you play, it's about how you play it.

Billy Corgan

Rock and Roll is still asking people like me to live up to the old guard's concept of what success is but it doesn't mean anything.

Billy Corgan

Rock in the mainstream culture has lost a lot of its mojo.

Billy Corgan

Saturn Return is just the return of your planets to their original position.

Billy Corgan

Sometimes people just like being around each other, and good things come out of that.

Billy Corgan

Somewhere between the intellectual idea of why we're attracted to certain things and the pragmatic reality is some form of ever-evolving truth.

Billy Corgan

Soon you won't even have the choice to live or die as you wish!

Billy Corgan

The deeper I get into my life as a musician, I'm discovering that it becomes less and less about other people, and more about what I want to do. And that's a good place to be.

Billy Corgan

The desire to hit a big home run is dominating the music business.

Billy Corgan

The funny thing about me that most people never really understand is that, at heart, I'm really a jock.

Billy Corgan

The great thing about rock n' roll is, if you want to fight - like, fight the system, fight the man, fight the government, fight the people in front of you - it's Don Quixote all over again. You're really chasing windmills.

Billy Corgan

The ideology of the Smashing Pumpkins was ultimately more valuable than the music of the Smashing Pumpkins. That's what critics can't put their finger on.

Billy Corgan

The things I'm guided to do are really strange to me.

Billy Corgan

There is something mighty suspicious about declaring an emergency for something that has yet to show itself to be a grand pandemic.

Billy Corgan

There's a difference between being a poseur and being someone who's so emotionally challenged they're kind of just doing their best to show you what they've got.

Billy Corgan

There's a lot of days where you feel forgotten.

Billy Corgan

There's nothing wrong with technology. It's when technology is the story and not the artist, that's the problem.

Billy Corgan

These days you're not just competing with the tedium, you're competing with the cellphone.

Billy Corgan

To be able to put your arms around 24 years of music, it's really fun.

Billy Corgan

To me, it's the folly of man to make God human.

Billy Corgan

To re-embrace what I once loved about music has been a warming process for me, because it's a good, earned feeling now.

Billy Corgan

Ultimately, running a band is about the relationships you have with people.

Billy Corgan

We need to get back to a level of social responsibility that we haven't seen for a long time.

Billy Corgan

We were in Japan once where they had 30 kinds of green tea. I thought there was one.

Billy Corgan

We've turned into a whining society.

Billy Corgan

Well, I'm known as a guitar-rock guy, you know? You're not supposed to play with synthesizers. This is not in the rulebook.

Billy Corgan

Well, all rock and roll is based in artifice.

Billy Corgan

What most people do is try to find a comfortable persona that they're in alignment with and the public likes and appreciates them for.

Billy Corgan

When I've tried to reinvent the wheel, I get bashed for not doing the familiar things.

Billy Corgan

When you actually like each other, it translates to the music.

Billy Corgan

Where is this great love for rock and roll that existed for 50 or 60 years?

Billy Corgan

Wrestling is one of the last truly rebellious American things left.

Billy Corgan

You could have a zillion Facebook followers. Those people don't buy records. It's about a hundred to one...Record companies, they don't have any money, so they see social media as the free marketing... So... 'Billy, light yourself on fire and stand upside down, and that'll market the record.'

Billy Corgan

You have to be willing to deal with the ups and downs of the music, the ups and downs of the audience.

Billy Corgan

You have to keep adapting to the times. If you kind of go with it, it can kind of fun.

Billy Corgan

You just reach a point sometimes with somebody where it just doesn't work.

Billy Corgan

You know Americans are obsessed with life and death and rebirth, that's the American Cycle. You know, awakening, tragic, horrible death and then Phoenix rising from the ashes. That's the American story, again and again.

Billy Corgan

You will never see the four original Pumpkins on stage ever again, unless it's a Hall of Fame thing. But you would never see a tour. There's so much damage, there's no way.

Billy Corgan

You're in a band 24 hours a day.

Billy Corgan

You've got to be ready to be in a great relationship.

Billy Corgan

Your basic person wants to talk about material culture, internet culture. I think about God, cats, nature.

Billy Corgan

This page is intentionally left blank

This page is intentionally left blank

This page is intentionally left blank

This page is intentionally left blank

This page is intentionally left blank